THE INQUISITION

A History From Beginning to End

Copyright © 2017 by Hourly History

Table of Contents

Introduction

In the Middle Ages, the Roman Catholic Church's organization of judiciary force against heresy was referred to as the Inquisition. While the most famous instance of investigation occurred in Spain, it was not the sole representation of the Inquisition during this time. The investigations ranged across the continent of Europe, the Americas, and spanned over seven hundred years. Much like the Crusades, an Inquisition could be enacted by either a papal decree, or by the local governing body such as a kingship, prince, or local clergy. These holy ecclesiastical courts were charged with rooting out heretical cults and countering the spread of non-orthodox movements such as the Cathars and the Waldensians in the early Middle Ages. These two movements that began in the south of France as well as northern Italy were the earliest challenges to the power of the Holy See in Rome.

The Inquisition began in earnest in A.D. 1184, and stretched its influence across the centuries, only to take its last breath in 1826 with its final execution. The office of the papacy held considerable sway in the creation of these tribunal courts that sought to expunge heretical thought that countered the Vatican's orthodoxy. After the first era of the Episcopal Inquisitions, dated from A.D. 1184 to A.D. 1230, the formation of the Papal Inquisitions expanded the powers and range of these judiciaries.

In the beginning, the court of the Inquisition was founded not to seek out heretics, but to deal with smaller claims and crimes against the Holy Church. Over time, and with the spread of unorthodox teachings, the Inquisition took on a greater scope. The ecclesiastical courts tried those accused through a Germanic process called accusatio—a process in which the accused was tried, and if found innocent, could press charges against their accusers. This right acted as a disincentive for accusers to level false claims against their peers. Eventually, however, this practice was replaced with a method called inquisitio, formulated within the ancient Roman Empire. Inquisitio did away with the disincentive and acted as a catalyst for the growing number of cases that ballooned during the latter Middle Ages with the birth of the Reformation. This change in judicial process complimented by growing dissent within the Christian faith would create a firestorm that would engulf the whole of Christendom for centuries.

The Inquisition of the Holy Roman Church could now spread across Europe taking up arms against several different sects. The first Inquisition and Crusade against the Cathars would breathe life into the dogmatic machine of orthodoxy. It was the precursor to the most famous of inquisitions in Spain. It would not begin to gasp for air until the 18th century, where it would finally succumb.

Whether one agrees with the methods or motive of the Inquisition, it cannot be disputed that these inquisitions were instrumental in developing the legal codes on which modern society is built. It may also have been the very reason why brutal torture and capital executions became such a controversial issue in Western society. The

Inquisition, for all its faults, became a central part of the creation of modern society.

Chapter One

Opposition to the Church

"Maybe you who condemn me are in greater fear than I who am condemned."

—Giordano Bruno

In today's popular culture, the Inquisition is thought of as the brutal and unjust slaughter of those who dared to stand up the titanic power of the Roman Catholic Church. When someone hears of the Inquisition, they imagine torture racks, burning witches at the stake, and trials that condemned national and ethnic heroes. While these things did occur throughout the various incarnation of the Inquisition, it does not properly represent the entire narrative. The Inquisition put a weapon and a shield in an ideological war that ranged from approximately the twelfth to the nineteenth century.

The words of Giordano Bruno encapsulate the very essence of the Inquisition—it was at its core motivated by fear; fear of change, fear losing power, and fear of secularization. In the beginning, during the birth of the Inquisition, the Catholic Church was a completely different institution, then it was during the final death knell of the Inquisition. With each Inquisition, the Catholic Church was facing a unique issue, and as such, each Inquisition had its own personality or characteristics. Because of this, it becomes difficult to define an organization that was active over a span of more than nine hundred years. In each Inquisition, the heretics were different, the lands were different, and those in control were separated by decades and sometimes, centuries.

To fully understand the Inquisition, one must first understand the scope of power and influence the Catholic Church maintained in the early Middle Ages and carried through the Renaissance. During these centuries, the Catholic Church was quite possibly the most powerful institution in the Western world. At the time of the first Inquisition, it is safe to say that no single nation or kingdom would have even thought of defying a papal order or decree. In A.D. 1100, the Catholic Church stood at the center of the Western world, everything and everyone bowed to its might and power. The power and influence of the Church had been bolstered by the spoils of the first campaign to recover the Holy Land of Jerusalem, called the Crusades.

This burst of religious fervor among European peasants, nobles, and princes was an obvious signal of just how much of a hold the Church had on the hearts and minds of the populace. Figures suggest that the First Crusade convinced over one hundred thousand Europeans to flock to the rallying call of the Catholic Church.

Even with this power, the Church feared the dilution of their dogma and potentiality of a schism of their influence over the populace. The men in power knew the simple fact that an idea could be exponentially more powerful than any army put on the field of battle. Heresy was the charge against all who spoke, acted, or plotted against the Holy Church of Rome. It is well known that those in power fear only one thing—the loss of said power. The greater the power, the greater the fear, and thus the Catholic Church had much to fear in a world that would struggle violently to wrest itself from the grasp of mighty Rome.

The First Crusade brought back wealth beyond measure, and with that wealth came ideas. Those who left their homes and ventured into the east, returned changed. While taking the Holy Land of Jerusalem, these men were exposed to a great many ideas that challenged what the Church had told them. When these men returned, they brought with them these ideas and shared them with their brethren. In a short time, those who once answered the call of the Catholic Church without question began to question every aspect of the narrative the Church had given them. These same men were sometimes men of power and influence, who spread their ideologies like wildfire among the people. It became obvious that these heretics needed to be stamped out, or the Catholic Church would suffer a collapse from within, as did the ancient Roman Empire.

The lesson of the fall of the Roman Empire was well learned by the Catholic Church. The very foundation on which the Church stood was the ruin of the ancient Roman Empire. They were no stranger to how hard one can fall when they have become too large for their support structures. If decay were to spread among the very smallest supports at the bottom and were allowed to reach the larger structures, then everything the Church had fought to gain would be undone. The Catholic Church needed a weapon to combat the rise in religious sectarianism, and that weapon would become the Inquisition. It would be forged of the same fear that forged the great Crusade, and it would inspire those loyal while terrifying those who opposed the indomitable and infallible word of Holy Rome.

Before A.D. 1100, the Catholic Church had little need for anything more persuasive than imprisonment or ecclesiastical proscription. Most would follow the laws and word of Rome uncontested. However, a rise in religious sectarianism would place the Church on its heels for the first time and force them into adopting more effective methods of rooting out and eliminating heretics. At the time, a large number of the clergy were against the use of torture in the case of punishment, as it did not fall in line with their idea of Christian values. However, by the time of the rise of Catharism and other sectarian groups throughout Europe, the clergy had changed the mind. In A.D. 1184, the Inquisition was born to combat the rising tide of ideologies that did not adhere to the rule of the Holy Church of Rome.

Over the next several centuries, the Inquisition would rise as a power that was feared by peasant and noble. It would be respected and vilified. It would set poignant examples before the public as a reminder that the final word rests with the Catholic Church of Rome. In the struggle to maintain a stranglehold on the only bastion of truth in Christendom, the Inquisition's grip would eventually begin to slip. Each finger the clergy stuck in the dike, would create another hole and soon enough the dam would break. Like the ancient Roman Empire, the Holy Roman Catholic Church would face the horde, and over time its power would decay and crumble under the weight of a free-thinking populace.

Chapter Two

The Conception of the Inquisition

"Kill them all. God will recognize his own."

—Arnaud Amalric

To understand why the Inquisition—or Inquisitions, a term better suited to explain the phenomenon—were so formative in the creation of modern society, one must understand the difference of ideas behind the warring parties. This war of ideas between small sects of Christianity and the greater whole of the Roman Catholic Church began with the return of the soldiers of the Second Crusade. The Crusades were similar in scope, in regard to how much the influence of the events would shape the power struggle within Europe. These surviving soldiers had seen the other side of the world, had encountered the horror of war and had their eyes opened to the corruption of the Holy See in Rome. Not only had they discovered that what they fought for was a corrupt institution, but that Christendom itself was not limited to the dogmatic approach of the orthodoxy. These men had traveled to the very birthplace of their faith, and in doing so had stumbled across an older, more inviting viewpoint—that of the freedom of the individual to decide. This core value, along with a denial of the sacred sacraments, was a direct contestation of both the power and validity of the Church of Rome.

It began with the Cathars in the south of France and the Waldensians of northern Italy. The Waldensians were the lesser problem, their primary issue being the accumulation of wealth by those in power. Though they also spoke against relics, saints, and the Eucharist, their denunciations were not quite as challenging as the Cathars in France. These two factions of early Protestantism began the tidal wave that would follow in the coming centuries of decent against Rome.

The Cathars, originally called the Albigensians, were a Christian sect that had ties to the soldiers that had returned from the Crusades. These soldiers appear to have been influenced by the teaching of the Manicheans or the Bogomils of Bulgaria. Though the soldiers returned to their homes abroad in France and England, it was the group of people from the south of France that would openly defy and denounce the teachings of the Holy Roman Church. The rise of Catharism was widespread, but most of the other sects had been wiped out in England and northern France. The sect in the south of France, however, had been protected by the southern nobles. This blanket of protection, and possibly their desire to avenge their brothers and sisters who had been wiped out or suppressed, provided the Cathars within southern France with a boldness that would be their undoing.

What did they preach to those who followed them? What did they believe that so stirred the venom of Rome? The Cathars were a sect of the Gnostic branch of Christianity, and as such, they believed in a dualistic version of the faith. They believed that there were two gods, one evil and one good. One god who created the physical and material world, and one who created the realm of the spirit. Coupled with their belief in the transmigration of souls, or reincarnation as it most commonly referred to, set them apart from the dogma being taught by Rome. The Cathars were also pacifists, and they renounced eating meat besides fish and placed a great deal of power and influence in the hands of women. Additionally, the Cathars preached an attitude of tolerance towards other religions, defied the Church's concept of marriage, and adhered only to the New Testament.

Despite these differences, the Catholics who lived in the same towns and cities as the Cathars showed tolerance and acceptance. Perhaps, had the Cathars not gone to such lengths to annoy and poke the Church they may have avoided an all-out confrontation with Rome.

The principles by which the Cathars lived their lives were in direct violation of the belief in Rome that there was only one god. This divide only grew as neither side was able to come to terms. Slowly the divide widened. Suppression began early, around the 1140s, with the Church declaring the faith heretical, but it wasn't until the Cathars openly stated their intention to form a counter-church in the south of France that the Church of Rome began to take them seriously.

The Cathars had openly called the Church in Rome corrupt, often stating in plain view that "the Church was full of ravening wolves and hypocrites" and "they worship the wrong god." Despite the Church's best efforts to denounce and suppress the Cathars in France, the movement spread. Within the south of France, there was a fire ready to be set ablaze. The climate was anti-establishment; the lower classes owned their land, the merchant and banking class held immense power, and the local folklore, spread by troubadours, solidified the populace into a force that boldly spoke against the tyranny and corruption of the Roman Church. The Church's retribution would be precise, and its revenge would be swift.

Chapter Three

The Episcopal and Papal Inquisitions

"With our hearts, we believe, and with our lips, we confess but one Church, not that of the heretics, but the Holy Roman Catholic and Apostolic Church, outside which we believe that no one is saved."

—Pope Innocent III

The first of the Medieval or Middle Age Inquisitions began with the Cathars of southern France. In A.D. 1184, Pope Lucius III issued the papal bull of Ad abolendam, to do away with the growing spread of Catharism. This decree marked the moment of the Inquisition's birth. The order placed the responsibility of seeking out and administering punishment of heretics to the local bishop. Twice a year, the bishop was charged to return to his home archdiocese and root out heretics.

Although the suppression began in A.D. 1147, the conflict between the Cathars, the French nobles, and the clergy did not reach its peak until after Pope Innocent III took power in A.D. 1198. Innocent attempted various methods of conversion and suppression but was frustrated at every turn by the Cathar resistance. No matter the method, the Cathars were firm in their resolve to create another church, one that taught their doctrine and not the doctrine of Rome.

Before the Inquisition was fully established, heresy was dealt with on the local level with little to no oversight by the Church. Because of the nature of medieval civil law and its intersection with Church law, the Catholic Church could not maintain control over what occurred in each trial. In many cases before the founding of the Inquisition, mob rule and uneducated princes were left to deal with local heretics as they saw fit. This lack of oversight led to a number of events that lent traction to the resistance of the various sects. Pope Lucius and some of his successors had hopes that the Inquisition could be a means to help heretics see falsity in their claims and return to the flock of the Church. This attempt to give heretics a chance to return to the faith seems at face value to be an honest attempt to eliminate proceedings that led to riots or unfounded executions. However, the Inquisition's task to restore heretics to their former faith was close to impossible to achieve. Additionally, abuse was rampant within the system of prosecution, in some cases with inquisitors embezzling the confiscated wealth of those accused of heresy. This corruption would only bolster the resolve of those who were resisting the Catholic Church.

Ultimately, the tenacity of the Cathars led to an order of excommunication from the Holy See. The order was issued with a declaration of the formation of a crusade against the Cathars and the French nobles who protected them. The war against the Cathars of France began in January A.D. 1208, with several northern houses marching on their southern brothers.

On July 22, 1209, approximately thirty thousand soldiers marched on the southern city of Béziers. They approached their enemy undetected by flying a flag of the Cathar resistance. When they had surrounded the town, they demanded that the two hundred Cathars who were living within the city be turned over to them. The Catholics of Béziers refused, stating that "they'd rather be flayed alive than to give up their brothers and sisters." The death knell of the Cathars occurred when the twenty thousand souls in the town of Béziers were put to the sword. This massacre at Béziers may be one of the key points in the history of the Inquisition. In no other Inquisition did the Church turn to such barbarity as they did with the Cathars.

Though the French nobles and leaders of the Cathar resistance were defeated shortly after the massacre at Béziers, the Cathar movement hung on for another century in the shadows of the Inquisition. The Crusaders had requested to return to their homes after the massacre at Béziers but were denied. Instead, they were forced by the Church to continue clearing out Cathars until southern France was free of their influence. In 1210, the same Crusaders surrounded the fortress of Minerve and created "the first great bonfire of heretics." Those who witnessed the fire stated that the condemned Cathars ran towards the fires as they were lit and threw themselves into the flames as a symbol of their resolve. Soon enough, the powers of the Cathar resistance in southern France had been defeated. Although the Cathars as an influential movement had fizzled out, they remained hidden and active in some areas for over a century with the last known Cathar prefectus being executed in 1321.

Chapter Four

The Hammer of Witches

"The deeds of witches are such that they cannot be done without the help of Devils."

—Heinrich Kramer

The period that extended from the fourteenth to the sixteenth century would be one of the darkest and most difficult times in European history. The people who lived through this era were troubled by more than poverty as had been the primary concern in the time before. They had to contend with the Black Death, a rampant plague that swept through Europe taking with it millions of souls in the process. On top of the plague, the Hundred Years War raged on for decades on end. The kingdoms of England and France tore western Europe apart with their blood feud which was fueled by their hunger for power. As if war and plague were not enough, the earth herself began to strike. In what was called the Little Ice Age, a gradual glaciation of the climate began to affect crops and create unpredictable weather. It was a perfect storm that would create the proper conditions for what would become a controversial era in the history of the Inquisition and that of the history of the world.

The farmers, peasants, and serfs of Europe were all dependent upon crops, harvests, and the predictability of the seasons. However, during this period, everything they knew, everything they had been taught by generations before was thrown out the window. If your children weren't dying from the plague, they were lost to war, or to starvation because of the changing climate. With literally every aspect of life delivering a punch to the gut, the citizens of Europe turned to the most common device used by man when times are trying, the scapegoat.

The superstitions of local folklore throughout Europe maintained that bad weather and bad luck were telltale signs of witchcraft. The practice of witchcraft can be traced back to pre-Christian Europe, where even the pagans themselves organized witch hunts from time to time, especially when times were hard. This superstition and the belief that bad luck and bad weather were signs of a witch's curse, was a difficult idea for the Catholic Church to dispel. The local folklore was often adopted by the Catholic Church to aid in the process of conversion. In fact, many of the deities that each region had previously worshiped had been transformed into saints as a way of easing the process. The long-standing belief of the Church in regard to witchcraft was that it was simply superstition and not a viable threat to the Church or its flock. The Medieval Church often distinguished between "white" and "dark" magic, only intervening in the case of malevolent use of dark magic.

In the cases of dark magic, the Church would often seek to produce a confession, followed by repentance and an assignment of charitable work within the community for the crime. Burning witches at the stake was not an official habit or procedure maintained by the Church in the first thirteen hundred years of Christianity in Europe. Many of the local folk practices were tied directly to the old religions and simply had a new Christian face stamped on the old ways. Bonfires were still lit at Midsummer, and other festivals were held to ward off bad weather, and the Church hardly ever lifted a finger to remove the old ways. Towards the later end of the era, things began to change within the populace, and the Church would have to adjust to appease and dispel the fear of the masses by taking up arms against whoever was to blame for everyone's misfortune.

It is important to note that throughout this period, although there were most certainly executions and torturous punishments dealt out to supposed witches, no one truly knows the extent to which the practice was applied. Some claim millions, despite the fact that the population of Europe during this period was unable to provide millions of deaths at the hands of witch hunters. But millions surely did fall to the perfect storm of fear, war, plague, and climate shifts.

Enter Heinrich Kramer, a German Catholic clergyman with an obsession with all things related to witchcraft. Kramer sought to elevate sorcery and all forms of witchcraft to a criminal status throughout Europe. In truth, this war of ideologies may even be tied to the remnants of the prior Inquisitions against various sects. His idea was that witches were no better than heretics and thus should be burned at the stake like the heretics. The crux of his beliefs centered upon how to find and torture witches and then how to properly unearth a confession. While his ideas were accepted widely by the common folk, many of the clergy and princes alike did not approve. Kramer often found his positions blocked politically. In response to this adversity, Kramer released his findings and beliefs in a book titled the *Malleus Maleficarum,* or the *Hammer of Witches.* This book would go on to spur superstitious belief in witches and lead to many witch hunts in the name of the Catholic Church.

Even though the Holy Roman Church never took an official position nor opened an Inquisition into the prosecution of witches on a large scale, many cases throughout this period were treated in the same manner. The true effect of the *Malleus Maleficarum* was that the Church began to sanction torture to produce confessions when interrogating and trying heretics of all kind. It may have taken decades, even centuries, but the Inquisition now had yet another tool to use against those who challenged the power and doctrine of the Church.

The famed case of Joan of Arc can be identified as a case of witchcraft. Joan of Arc, a French woman who took up arms against the English in her home country of France was also tried by the Church and the powers that be. Alternately called the Maid of Orleans, Joan of Arc became a hero of the Hundred Years War when she led her countrymen to a series of pivotal victories against the English. What drew the attention of the Church was that Joan claimed that she received instructions from angelic voices that told her how to defeat the armies of the English. It was no surprise that a woman leading men would irritate and challenge the official stance of the Church, but also that a woman could be in direct communication with heavenly hosts was an automatic red flag for the Church. By 1430, only a year after her rise from simple peasant girl to a military commander, the Church struck her down. Joan of Arc was executed for the heretical offense of cross-dressing and impersonating a man, as a woman could not hold the station of a military commander. Joan was burned at the stake, but quickly became a martyr for the French national cause that would later deliver victory for the French in the Hundred Years War. Officially, the Church would remand its position and declare her a martyr only sixteen years later.

Despite the Church's ability to admit its wrongdoing in the case of Joan of Arc, the darkest periods of the Inquisition were yet to come.

Chapter Five

The Spanish Inquisition

"The Inquisition was not born out of a desire to crush diversity or oppress people; it was rather an attempt to stop unjust executions. Yes, you read that correctly. Heresy was a crime against the state. Roman law in the Code of Justinian made it a capital offense. Rulers, whose authority was believed to come from God, had no patience for heretics."

—Thomas Madden

With each step taken in the previous centuries, the Catholic Church had opened the door for a truly massive spectacle to occur. The Inquisition was more powerful than ever before, and heresy had thrived despite its best efforts. Now more than ever before, heretics were emerging from seclusion. Cases against heretics, Jews, Muslims, witches, high profile nobles, bishops, even kings and queens, were all becoming commonplace. Europe was engulfed in strife, neighbor betrayed neighbor, and no one was truly safe from persecution. But no country in Europe was more prone to detonate into madness than Spain.

The kingdom of Spain had undergone change after change in recent years as the balance of power shifted from Moorish Muslim control to that of Catholic rule in the form of Ferdinand II of Aragon and Isabella I of Castile. Through conquest and shrewd negotiation, Ferdinand had reclaimed the whole of the Iberian Peninsula, save Portugal, by the end of his reign. It was a turbulent time, and although the law of the land had been tolerance of other religions in previous centuries, tolerance began to dwindle under the rule of Ferdinand and Isabella.

The Moors had always supported an official stance of tolerance to the Jews and the Christians under their rule. As such, nearly everyone in the Iberian Peninsula coexisted with others of differing faiths. Throughout the previous iterations of the Inquisition in other kingdoms, there had yet to be an official Inquisition in Spain. The Episcopal leaders had been left to handle heresy as they saw fit. Given that the land was markedly different, the episcopates did little when compared to inquisitors elsewhere in Europe.

Across Europe, in the thirteenth and fourteenth centuries, there was a mass expulsion of the Jewish populations. The English expelled their populations in 1290, and the French followed suit in 1309. Meanwhile, Spain had tolerated and even accepted many Jews into positions of great merit. However, centuries of tolerance were about to be thrown out the window. By the summer of 1391 things began to come to a head as anti-Semitic sentiment had spread deeply into the heart of Spain. The anti-Jewish riots broke out first in Barcelona, and in just a few short months the unrest spread to cities like Seville,

Toledo, Cordoba, and Mallorca. During this time, nearly every Jewish population within Spain either fled or rapidly began to convert to Christianity. These converts were called conversos, and despite their willingness to convert to Christianity they were still held to be a lower class in the eyes of the public and the law. It is said that during this period over two hundred thousand Jews converted or began to hide their religion from the public eye. Sadly, despite the mass conversion, the conversos were treated no better than they had been. In many cases, mass forced baptisms occurred.

This pressure on the Jewish community would not cease, by 1478 tension between Jews and Christians would boil over. With fear of uprisings among the Jewish populations, Ferdinand and Isabella requested a papal bull to institute an Inquisition to aid in re-converting or punishing the conversos that had returned to practicing Judaism. In 1480, their suspicions were confirmed when an uprising threatened to overthrow the local government in Seville. That would be the final straw. Ferdinand pressed the Pope and threatened to dissolve the bonds between the Inquisition in Spain and the direction of Rome. In November 1478, Pope Sixtus IV issued a papal bull that gave monarchs the power to appoint inquisitors within their kingdoms. It was largely believed that Pope Sixtus relinquished this control to allay fears that he was too soft on the New Christians.

By 1481 the first auto-da-fe was held, and six people were executed by way of burning at the stake. In 1492, the Inquisition had spread to eight other Castilian cities. Pope

Sixtus IV decried the methods of the Inquisition and issued a decree prohibiting the expansion of the Inquisition into Aragon. His concerns were largely well-founded.

In 1483, it was clear that Ferdinand and Isabella desired to wrest control of the Inquisition from the soft hands of Pope Sixtus IV. The pair of monarchs appointed the hardline Dominican Friar Tomas de Torquemada, known for his extreme methods. Despite the Pope's concerns, Torquemada assumed the mantle of Inquisitor General, making him one of the most powerful men in Europe. Shortly after that, Andalusia saw all of its Jewish population expelled.

In 1484, the newly appointed Pope Innocent III tried to bring the Inquisition back under the control of Rome by allowing for those convicted of heresy to appeal to Rome, effectively circumventing the Inquisition in Spain. His success was short-lived as Ferdinand again threatened to sever the connection. Shortly after, the murder of an inquisitor in Aragon swayed public opinion away from pity for the conversos. With both the public and the monarchy behind them, the Inquisition rolled on in Spain.

It is estimated that during the time that Tomas de Torquemada was in power in Spain approximately two thousand souls were put to death, a great many only after surviving excruciating torture at the hands of a bloodthirsty Inquisition. An overwhelming majority of those convicted and imprisoned were Jewish conversos.

The Inquisition, although focused on the Jewish populations, was active in a number of other realms. Moriscos, or forcibly converted Muslims, were targeted in large numbers. Protestants were often tried and sent to prison, to combat the Protestant Reformation. In an effort to bolster the Counter-Reformation, censorship took center stage. The Inquisition created indexes of legal books and codices that could be owned by the general population. Witchcraft, bigamy, sodomy, Freemasonry, and any ideology that may contradict the Catholic Church were placed under the microscope of the Inquisition, though none of these groups were as heavily targeted as the Jews.

In some cases, the Inquisition even saw landfall in the New World. Both the Mexican and Peruvian Inquisitions were the long arms of the Spanish Inquisition's power. By the late 1700s, the Inquisition was also put to work suppressing nationalist agendas in foreign colonies to prevent upheavals like those seen in British America and the French Revolution in neighboring France.

The Spanish Inquisition did not see its final days until it was disbanded in 1834. Regardless of the brutality and force used by the monarchs and the Inquisition, it can be stated that because of their effectiveness in maintaining a stranglehold on their population, Spain was able to succeed in many arenas where other states were unable.

Chapter Six

The Portuguese Inquisition

"Goa is sadly famous for its inquisition, equally contrary to humanity and commerce. The Portuguese monks made us believe that the people worshiped the devil, and it is they who have served him."

—Voltaire

While the Spanish Inquisition often is the most notable or most famous, the Portuguese and Goan Inquisitions may have been equally as terrible in scope. The Portuguese Colonial Empire stretched across the continents of the Americas, Africa, and Asia with colonies in Brazil, Cape Verde, and Goa. Although their reach was much smaller in size, the ambition of the Portuguese may have rivaled the Spanish. A contemporary of the Spanish and Roman Inquisitions, the Portuguese Inquisition dealt with some similarities including the expulsion of Jews. By and large, the Inquisition in Portugal focused its attention on the Jewish populations that had flooded their cities as they fled from Spain. Outside of the borders of Portugal, the Goan Inquisition and other varied branches of the Portuguese Inquisition met challenges that were utterly foreign to other Inquisitions occurring in Europe.

It should be noted that at first, the Portuguese wanted no part of the Inquisition, despite incredible pressure from the monarchs of Spain. However, by 1497, in an effort to solidify relations between the two nations, King Manuel 1 married Isabella of Aragon, and after her death, he was betrothed to her younger sister Maria. As part of the marriage contract, the Spanish monarchs insisted that a clause is adopted that allowed the expansion of the Inquisition into Portugal and to expel all the Jewish refugees that had fled Spain for Portugal.

The Inquisition in Portugal was largely handicapped initially. For several years, King Manuel I stalled its progress and hindered its influence, due to the entrenched wealth of the Jewish communities of his kingdom. Spanish pressure was great and eventually King Manuel I ordered the conversion of the Jews within his kingdom. His order of conversion was only half-serious as he stated that the order was not to be investigated for at least two decades. Despite his efforts to outmaneuver the Spanish, in 1506 a pair of Spanish Dominican Friars instigated a mob in Lisbon to violence. Several hundred Jewish conversos, called Marranos in Portugal, were killed. It is estimated that after this massacre tens of thousands of Jews began to flee persecution in Portugal—leaving for England, Amsterdam, and some to Asian Goa. The official figures of the Portuguese Inquisition may be less than half the numbers of those put to death in Spain. However, this does not fully represent its extent. The largest and most influential of the Portuguese Inquisitions was the Inquisition in Goa. When the Inquisition was disbanded in Goa, all records were lost or destroyed, making a clear picture of the entire puzzle nearly impossible to decipher.

The Island of Goa became a colonial possession of Portugal after the Portuguese were granted the rights to all trade in Asia by the papal decree of Pope Nicholas V. After four decades, it appeared that the Portuguese were not interested in the conversion of the indigenous populations. In an effort to expand the influence of the Church in Asia, the Pope sent missionaries from the Society of Jesus to aid in conversion. Alms for the poor were distributed to encourage the conversion of the Hindu population, but many continued to practice their old religion in secret. It wasn't until St. Francis Xavier appealed to the Pope for aid that an Inquisition was formally started in Goa.

St. Francis Xavier penned a letter to the Pope detailing his observances of the local culture. Needless to say, his opinions and views on the local culture painted the Hindu culture and people in an extremely negative and dishonest light. In his letter, he described, "The Hindus are an unholy race. They are liars and cheats to the very backbone. Their idols are black—as black as black can be— ugly and horrible to look at, smeared with oil and smell in an evil manner."

The first inquisitors began by first banning any open practice of the Hindu faith under penalty of death. Their focus then shifted to persecute the Sephardic Jews that had fled mainland Portugal. Anti-Hindu laws were enacted to keep the Hindu population under the subjugation of the Church. Hindus were ordered to gather periodically to listen to sermons and in some cases forced to publicly refute their old religion. The segregation of Christians and Hindu populations began to widen the divide between those who maintained their old religion and those who were forcibly converted.

At first, the Inquisition did not have the desired effect. Many Hindus simply fled the persecution of the tribunals to the mainland or Muslim-controlled territories. Another unintended consequence was that a large number of Portuguese nationals expatriated, offering their services to various sultans and Indian kings. In 1566, an order was issued that condemned the building, repairing of, and use of Hindu temples in Goa. A campaign to raze the Hindu temples of Goa began in 1567, and over three hundred temples were torn down. This action was only the beginning of what would become a systematic cleansing of the Hindu populations of Goa. Sacred books were banned, burned, and confiscated. Hindu marriage rituals were banned, as well as statues and sacred rituals using oils and incense under penalty of death. Virtually everything that represented their religion was torn away from them, down to their own language Konkani, which would later be banned.

The influence of the Goan Inquisition would even reach mainland India in Kerala where smaller sects of Syrian Christians were persecuted for allegedly practicing Nestorian heresy. Some sources claim that the brutality of the Portuguese was equal to or greater than the force employed by the Spanish. Perhaps this is why the Inquisition destroyed the records at its disbandment. If local sentiment is any indication, there is no love lost between the Hindu people of Goa and the Catholic Church.

Chapter Seven

The Roman Inquisition

"I do not feel obliged to believe that the same God who has endowed us with sense, reason, and intellect has intended us to forgo their use."

—Galileo Galilei

A contemporary of the Spanish and Portuguese Inquisitions, the Roman Inquisition was stationed in Italy. The formal name of the body was the Supreme Sacred Congregation of the Roman and Universal Inquisition. Stationed primarily within the Holy See, the Roman Inquisition maintained an attitude that was more bureaucratic than the Spanish or Portuguese Inquisitions. The formal policy of the Roman Inquisition was that of mitigation, prevention, and control. Put simply; the Roman Inquisition was more concerned with how the public at large saw the Inquisition and the Church. It was more visible and dealt with higher profile cases than its more brutal counterparts.

Initiated in the latter half of the sixteenth century, the Roman Inquisition sought to expand the definition of heresy to broaden the control of the Church over popular belief. The Church had many problems throughout Europe, especially with the ever-growing popularity of the

Protestant Reformation. Originally, the office of the Roman Inquisition was forged to deal with the matter of heresy including Protestantism, blasphemy, witchcraft, and sorcery among other things. However, as the Renaissance began to produce a more open and inviting environment for free thought, the Church felt it necessary to expand the definition of heresy. This expansion included but was not limited to the prosecution of love magic, alternate religious beliefs, and alternate religious doctrines.

Created to combat the spread of Protestantism, the Roman Inquisition also presided over cases of a more secular nature. Many of the prosecuted were scientists whose study of the cosmos began to challenge the narrative of the Church. With the rise of Pope Pius V in 1566, the Inquisition began to reassess its rather lax stance and went on the offensive. By the following year, they had imprisoned and executed a young theologian by the name of Pietro Carnesecchi, an advocate of Lutheranism and an example to all those who would speak publicly of their displeasure with Rome. This message was clear; all who challenged or taught a different doctrine than Rome would be harshly punished.

One of the primary tools available to the Roman Inquisition was the *Index Librorum Prohibitorum*, a list of forbidden books. Any book or publication that was found to be heretical, anti-clerical, or unfairly satirized the Church was formally banned from the Roman Catholic Church. This list was held by a local ordinary, to whom the local congregation would consult before purchasing or reading material that may lead them astray. It was an effective way of maintaining a stranglehold on the hearts and minds of the Catholic faith while stunting the spread of heretical ideologies that had become rampant during the Renaissance. Included in the *Index* were many works by esteemed and bold scientists, particularly those who claimed that the Church was wrong.

The advent of a heliocentric theory of the cosmos was one of the hot-button issues the Roman Inquisition faced. In 1543, Nicolaus Copernicus published *On the Revolutions of the Heavenly Spheres*. The book was a revolutionary model of the solar system which stated that the sun was the center of the universe and not the Earth. Although Copernicus cited the ancient Greeks who were well respected, the Church found that his works were not only heretical but also erroneously devoid of faith. In 1616, his work *On the Revolutions of the Heavenly Spheres* was added to the *Index Librorum Prohibitorum*. Despite the Church's official position, Copernicus' work spread to other great minds who would build upon his work. Copernicus died shortly after publishing his book on heliocentrism and thus escaped the punishment of the Church in Rome. Those who followed in his footsteps would not be as lucky.

Giordano Bruno was a Dominican Friar with a taste for free thought and books that would have been listed in the *Index Librorum Prohibitorum*. A monastic youth, his taste for free thinking led him down a path that would irritate the Church. Troubled by an inability to keep a low profile, Bruno ruffled feathers wherever he went. In

England, he was supposedly accepted into the Hermetic circle together with the famous John Dee. In France, Dee's papers drew ill favor. This poet, mathematician, and philosopher held many ideas that were labeled heresy; including the transmigration of souls, or reincarnation, the infinite nature of the universe, and his attachments to pantheism. In 1592, Bruno was arrested in Venice under the charges of blasphemy and heresy. His trial would be long and his imprisonment harsh. Bruno's stubborn nature would be his undoing, as in 1600 he was convicted of heresy and sentenced to death for refusing to recant his beliefs in the plurality of worlds and other key aspects of his philosophy. In February 1600, Bruno's tongue was removed and he was hung naked in the city square and burned at the stake. All of Bruno's works were placed in the *Index Librorum Prohibitorum* after his death. The case of Giordano Bruno did well to deter some, but the enticement of free thought was rampant in Europe.

Enter one of the most famous people to ever be tried by the Inquisition, Galileo Galilei. Galileo was an astronomer, philosopher, mathematician, engineer, and physicist whose championing of the Copernican theory of heliocentrism would become one of the most intriguing and high-profile cases of the Roman Inquisition. The primary concern of the Church in regard to heliocentrism was that it, directly and across multiple points, contradicted what Holy Scripture held to be true. Galileo was at first supported far and wide by Catholic sects like the Jesuits. But his tenacity in defending his work from the Church's slander ended up seeming like direct attacks on Pope Urban VIII. With his support base gone, Galileo would be tried and found guilty of suspected heresy. Galileo was forced to recant his positions and was placed under house arrest for the rest of his natural life. While it may not seem as harsh as the trial of Giordano Bruno and others before him, the trial against Galileo would be historically viewed as a mistake. It would take the Church over two hundred years to lift the ban on Galileo's works, and over four hundred years for them to admit the error they had made in condemning a man who was so instrumental in the scientific revolution.

Though the Roman Inquisition put fewer people to death when compared to its contemporary counterparts, it was no less remiss in its sheer drive to control the hearts and minds of the people of Europe. It would take many hundreds of years before the Catholic Church would be able to formally declare that the actions against the scientific titans of the Renaissance were ill-founded.

Chapter Eight

The End of the Inquisition

"The greatest tragedy in the history of Christianity was neither the Crusades nor the Reformation nor the Inquisition, but rather the split that opened up between theology and spirituality at the end of the Middle Ages."

—Hans Urs von Balthasar

The spread of free thought and growing nationalism gradually began to decay the power of the Catholic Church. At the height of power, the Inquisition had wielded a powerful weapon in the fight against heresy. But during the last three centuries, the Inquisitions in Spain, Portugal, Rome, and elsewhere dwindled. The Medieval Inquisition was long gone, the Portuguese Inquisition was the next to follow in 1821 after a stretch of two hundred and eighty-five years. The Spanish Inquisition would be the next, disbanded in 1834 after three hundred and fifty-six years. The Roman Inquisition was the last to be dissolved, although it still exists in a form today. In 1860, the Roman Inquisition was informally abolished, although there was still a contingent that operated in its stead. In 1908, the body was renamed to The Sacred Congregation of the Holy Office and again changed in 1965 to the Congregation for the Doctrine of Faith.

The fight against the dissolution of the power they gained in the Middle Ages had scourged the Church's reputation. It may have held the problems at bay for a few centuries, but it did not stop the tide. Slowly the methods of the Inquisition were banned or became wholly unpopular according to both clergy and congregation. The fight was over, and the Catholic Church had lost. One question remained, had it gained anything?

With the last execution happening in Spain in 1826, it can be argued that the Inquisition succeeded in one of their tasks; to eliminate unnecessarily cruel punishment, torture, and execution. Throughout the Middle Ages, the Renaissance, even clear into the nineteenth century, secular punishments were found to be crueler by the eyes of the Church. Many of the hundreds of thousands if not millions that were put on trial were sentenced to terms of service, or simply to recant their beliefs. The Inquisition may have a tarnished reputation, but its intervention during troubled times may have been a shield for the people against rulers whose methods were often found to be more extreme. By the mid to late nineteenth century, historians began to rummage through the surviving court records. Gradually, they began to use the patient sight of history and were able to gather a different picture of the Inquisition over time.

Overall it has been posited that the Inquisition as a whole does not solely rest on the shoulders of one Pope or one Church, but rather on the Medieval European superstructure. Many of the Inquisitions were formed at the behest of heads of state. Many of the singular cases were not initiated by bishops or inquisitors, but by neighbors and family members. As the Inquisition faded into memory and was no longer a threat, it became easier for people to see the Inquisition for what it truly was. It became clear that the Inquisition brought with it unholy terrors, but it also brought forth good, in the form of many of our legal codes of conduct today. Its unique and barbaric tortures became the predecessors of techniques that have hardly faded into history but rather morphed into more sophisticated techniques that we as humans have used contemporarily.

The Inquisition may have been disbanded, but its influence stretches far beyond time, as a reminder of absolute power, as a tarnishing mark, and as a historical period that aids us in creating a better future. The Inquisition cannot be labeled as wholly bad nor wholly good, although opponents and apologetics would make cases for both. It was instead an amalgam, a potent mixture of evil and good.

Appearances in popular media like the comedic skits on *Monty Python and the Flying Circus* have kept this magnanimous event in the public consciousness. More appearances have occurred that have painted it in both negative and positive lights, such as the bloody scenes of the Grand Inquisitor Torquemada in films like the *Fountain*. Unfortunately, the long arc of history has shadowed many of the actions of the Inquisition in its murky waters.

Chapter Nine

Shades of the Inquisition in Modern Society

"Looking at the Inquisition . . . in its higher dimensions it was animated not by greed or hope of gain or love of power, though these were never absent, by the fervent conviction that all must subscribe to some ultimate truth."

—Cullen Murphy

The Medieval and subsequent Inquisitions brought forth weapons and machines of torture like the Judas Chair, the Head Vice, and the famed rack. These implements among other forms of execution like disembowelment are no longer used in modern society. Nor do we publicly shame or force people to recant in front of their peers. Trials for witchcraft and sodomy are mostly a thing of the distant past. So how does this unbelievable event still impact our society today?

In many ways, it acts as a warning sign to humanity. Modern society is a melting pot of ideas, ethnicities, religions, and cultures thanks to the globalization that has occurred over the past two or three centuries. Events like the Crusades happen today, in different forms, like the Islamic Jihad, while events like the Inquisition are echoed in the torture methods used in American prisons like Abu Ghraib. By and large, the Inquisition served to create and sophisticate the legal codes that are still used today. Based on Roman legal codes, the Roman Catholic church may have provided modern society with an innate protection against the abuse of power by the State or any other governing body. Some argue this point today.

Despite modern political climates, the modern world is far more accepting of people of different values. Gone are the days of persecuting Jewish or Muslims populations at large. Cases of bigotry are still common, but mass expulsions and executions are now a distant memory. We as humans learn from our past mistakes, and over time the Catholic Church has apologized and recanted the behavior of its predecessors. Events like the Crusades, the Reformation, and the Inquisition stand as warning signs for humanity today. They urge us to be careful and cautious before adopting attitudes of fear, anger, and resentment towards our fellow brothers and sisters, despite their beliefs. They ask us not to repeat the same mistakes our ancestors did, by accusing each other of being a witch or a heretic. Not only have our legal codes served as a protection, but some have argued that fear of a recurrence keep humanity in check.

Chapter Ten

The Truth in the Numbers

"The secrets of slavery are concealed like those of the Inquisition."

—Harriet Ann Jacobs

Many claims have been put forward over the course of the historical study of the Inquisition. Some claim that there were mere thousands of executions, others that the death toll reached millions. The truth is that no one is certain of just how many people were put to death by the Inquisition, formally or informally. Not all records from the centuries of activity have survived the ages, some have been purposefully destroyed as in the case of the Inquisition in Goa, and others have just fallen to decay. Erring on the side of accuracy and caution, it does not appear that millions were put to death by the Church alone. Millions did indeed die horrible deaths in the Middle Ages, from starvation, war, and plague, but millions were not burned at the stake, by the Church. It can, however, be stated that the Church's official positions may have led to the deaths of millions at other hands. Witch hunts, pogroms, and ethnic cleansing were all common and rampant during the Medieval periods, but the majority were carried out locally, without the consent of the Holy Church of Rome.

Events like the Inquisition have raised incredible distrust of the Catholic Church over the centuries, markedly by those of the Protestant faith. Most of the surviving records are those of the Church themselves. Could the Church have faked, or fudged the numbers to appear more appealing? It is hard to see clearly. The number of executions that most historians agree upon seem to range in the thousands.

The first Inquisition ended with the absolute and utter destruction of an entire town, with figures ranging near twenty thousand. There were undoubtedly more Cathars and Waldensians put to death during this period, but not all were the fault of the Church. Many heads of state can be implicated in the deaths of the first Inquisition.

It's nearly impossible to grasp the number of deaths because of the witch trials of the Middle Ages. Remarkably, the numbers of the Spanish Inquisition are most likely to be the most accurate. Bordering on two thousand people put to death, the numbers tell us that the historically most brutal of the iterations of the Inquisition only executed one percent of those they put on trial. It must also be mentioned that the number of people put to death is not a proper representation of the scope of the atrocities committed. These figures do not reflect the number of people tortured, harassed, or driven from their homes.

The numbers of the Inquisition in Portugal were much smaller, ranging from about six to seven hundred executed. However, the largest activity in this arena happened abroad in Goa, to which we are not able to properly deduce the extent, due to the records being destroyed. Many local indigenous Hindu people still claim that this number was in the thousands.

What can be deduced by further study of the numbers? Using common sense, we can state that millions of people were affected by this formative event in our history as a species. Countless were indeed affected by the trying nature of the Medieval Period, and many lost their lives to war, plague, the Inquisition, or displacement. It must be noted that these factors came together to create a massive upheaval that shaped humanity forever.

Conclusion

What can be learned about the Inquisition that may help impede such an event from occurring again? Certainly, in modern society, there is little place for such an organization. However, the old proverb that history repeats itself has proven to be rather true. At its core, the Inquisition and the period that it thrived in were founded on fear—fear of the unknown, and fear of what was different. This fear was hastened along its destructive path by major events that created the perfect environment for a persecutory body like the Inquisition to thrive. The Black Death had already crippled every aspect of European life in between the first Episcopal and Papal Inquisitions and those that followed. Conflicts like the Hundred Years War between England and France brought a large portion of western Europe to its knees. Meanwhile, the Protestant Reformation engulfed all of Germany in a power struggle between the State and the Church. While that spread to virtually every corner of Europe, the Little Ice Age doomed crops. An unhappy public combined with monarchs and aristocrats who fear to lose their power can make for a disastrous mix. Neighbor would turn on trusted neighbor. Once things turned bad, people looked for a scapegoat, someone to blame.

The Inquisition was a war of ideas. Its first battle would be over what Christianity would be in Medieval Europe. The Cathars were the first group of freethinkers that dared to challenge the sacred word and law of Holy

Rome. The Cathars were unique from all other groups that would follow in their martyred footsteps. They were smaller than other groups, and yet their voices were so loud, that it drove the Church to lengths that it never again attempted. When the news reached Pope Innocent III that twenty thousand people, men, women, and children were put to the sword, it must have been quite similar to Harry S. Truman after the atomic bomb was let loose on Nagasaki. Only two hundred Cathars were put to death that day, while the remainder were loyal Catholics. What kind of fear could drive something to cut at its own body in such a manner? Many assumptions can be made as to why the Inquisition began this way, but it is unclear whether the largest slaughter of the Inquisition was politically motivated or if madness had truly won the day. In rooting out and destroying the Cathars and other groups like them, the Inquisition developed into a formidable agency, armed with new methods of controlling the hearts and minds of the public.

The acquisition of torture as a method of procuring confessions would be a key moment in the history of the Church's Grand Inquisition. It would become the sword that the people feared and to which they bowed. The rack, the wheel, the head vice, and countless other methods would be developed to impress and shock the public into submission. Witches, heretics, Jews, Protestants, indigenous peoples, and even the clergy themselves would all be subject to the horrors created in the name of the Church.

The suppression of other ideas would begin within the religious theater, but would later move into secular arenas. Persecution became coveted by monarchs as a way to maintain control over ambitious nobles or to root out populations that dreamt of revolution. In Spain, it was used to cull the Jewish population which had drawn the ire of many Christians due to their success. In Goa, Mexico, Peru, and other colonies, it was used to quell indigenous populations. In France, it was used against heroes like Joan of Arc, and against revolutionists. In Italy, it attempted to quell the brightest and most gifted people of the Renaissance. Galileo, Bruno, Copernicus, Kepler, Newton, and many more had their work impeded or silenced by the Church. Imagine the world today where books were banned. Had the Church succeeded in silencing these radical ideas we may have been sitting in a very different world. In fact, you may not even have been reading the facts presented within this book.

Though there were thousands if not more that died at the hands of the Inquisition, there were many constructive aspects that came from this dark period in human history. As mentioned before, the Inquisition was founded on a principle of providing a more amicable, just process of litigation. Medieval punishments were often cruel, barbaric, and utterly unjustified. Crimes like fornication were often met with a prominent branding on one's forehead. Imagine if, in today's world, a young teenage girl was struck with a hot iron because she dared to make a mistake or worse, to love someone. It was this leniency, provided by the more reasonable minds within the Catholic Church at the time that has shaped and molded our modern justice systems.

While this was one aim of the Inquisition, so was the ideology of the ends justifying the means. This ideology is still alive today in the national security prisons that torture terrorists to preserve the common good. Whether or not one these methods are morally defensible in modern times is still up for debate. But in Medieval times with a society that was constantly teetering on the brink of destruction, maintaining order by providing a unified and singular idea of what society should be like, may have been the single greatest thing the Inquisition did. This stability provided Europe with the ability to create such wonders as the Reformation, the Renaissance, and the Enlightenment. Despite the fact that the Church railed against these changing ideas when they arose, it does not take a great deal of imagination to see that the actions of the Church may have provided the proper environment for progress to succeed.

Some people might argue that harsh measures are needed to provide the proper environment for progress to take root. Much like a wildfire clears the way for new growth in a forest. While it is morally reprehensible to suggest another Inquisition should be necessary to catapult humanity into the next phase of our growth, at least in the Western World, it is not so mad to say that another will arise. Perhaps it already has. With travel bans on ethnic populations being a reality in parts of today's world, it echoes the anti-Semitic behaviors of Medieval Europe. We must stay vigilant and ask ourselves if we do not see a little bit of the Inquisition in modern society if we are to avoid repeating history and making the same mistakes all over again.

Printed in Great Britain
by Amazon

44960735R00029